Our Lady

by Charles V. Lacey

with a preface by

Rev. Raymond P. Lawrence

ACTA
ASSISTING CHRISTIANS TO ACT
PUBLICATIONS

By arrangement with
Benziger Publishing Company

Copyright © 1926, 1954 by Benziger Brothers, Inc. Printed in the U.S.A.
Nihil Obstat. John M.A. Fearns, S.T.D., Censor Librorum
Imprimatur. +Francis Cardinal Spellman, Archbishop of New York
New York, September 30, 1954

Rosary Novenas

PREFACE

MONSIGNOR BENSON, in one of his early novels, gave us a beautiful explanation of the Rosary. An old nun is trying to make the devotion clear to a young Protestant girl. The enquirer asks:

"How can prayers said over and over again like that be any good?"

Mistress Margaret was silent for a moment.

"I saw young Mrs. Martin last week," she said, "with her little girl in her lap. She had her arms around her mother's neck, and was being rocked to and fro; and every time she rocked she said 'Oh, mother.' "

"But, then," said Isabel, after a moment's silence, "she was only a child." " 'Except ye become as little children—' " quoted Mistress Margaret softly—"you see, my Isabel, we are nothing more than children with God and His Blessed Mother. To say, 'Hail Mary, Hail Mary,' is the best way of telling her how much we love her. And, then, this string of beads is like Our Lady's girdle, and her children love to finger it, and whisper to her. And then we say our Our Fathers too; and all the while we are talking, she is showing us pictures of her dear Child, and we look at all the great things

He did for us, one by one; and then we turn the page and begin again."

Those who have profited most from the Rosary are the ones who have thus understood it. With hearts full of love they have rested close by the side of our heavenly Mother; and, whispering words of endearment to her, they have gazed the while at those wonderful pictures which the changing mysteries recall, seeing always something new and beautiful. And when they have come to the end of the picture-book, with the insatiable interest of a child, they have gone back to the beginning and turned every page over again.

In the devotions which are offered in this little book, the prayers to be said at the beginning of each decade set before the mind those wonderful pictures in a simple and striking way. It is as if someone stood at our side to point out the beautiful and interesting things which by ourselves we might have missed. And then, in order that our seeing may not be profitless, we are led on at the end to ask for that grace which the mystery suggests. Surely, even apart from the making of the novenas, we must feel that this is the best method of reciting the rosary.

The devotion which this little brochure explains, should do much to spread this practice. It combines three things which are dear to God in a very remarkable scheme: frequent Communion, the practice of the virtues, and devotion to Mary in the Rosary. One who will carry it out faithfully will have besieged Heaven in a way that must make him heard.

REV. RAYMOND P. LAWRENCE

ORIGIN AND METHOD

THIS devotion, which the author has called the "Rosary Novenas to Our Lady," is of comparatively recent origin.

"In an apparition of Our Lady of Pompeii, which occurred in 1884 at Naples, in the house of Commander Agrelli, the heavenly Mother deigned to make known the manner in which she desires to be invoked.

"For thirteen months Fortuna Agrelli, the daughter of the Commander, had endured dreadful sufferings and torturous cramps; she had been given up by the most celebrated physicians. On February 16, 1884, the afflicted girl and her relatives commenced a novena of Rosaries. The Queen of the Holy Rosary favored her with an apparition on March 3rd. Mary, sitting upon a high throne, surrounded by luminous figures, held the divine Child on her lap, and in her hand a Rosary. The Virgin Mother and the holy Infant were clad in gold-embroidered garments. They were accompanied by St. Dominic and St. Catherine of Siena. The throne was profusely decorated with flowers; the beauty of Our Lady was marvelous.

"Mary looked upon the sufferer with maternal tenderness, and the patient saluted her with the words: 'Queen of the Holy Rosary, be gracious to me; restore me to health! I have already prayed to thee in a novena, O Mary, but have not yet experienced thy aid. I am so anxious to be cured!'

" 'Child,' responded the Blessed Virgin, thou hast invoked me by various titles and hast always obtained favors from me. Now, since thou hast called me by that title so pleasing to me, 'Queen of the Holy Rosary,' I can no longer refuse the favor thou dost petition; for this name is most precious and dear to me. Make three novenas, and thou shalt obtain all.'

"Once more the Queen of the Holy Rosary appeared to her and said, 'Whoever desires to obtain favors from me should make three novenas of the prayers of the Rosary, and three novenas in thanksgiving.'

"This miracle of the Rosary made a very deep impression on Pope Leo XIII, and greatly contributed to the fact that in so many circular letters he urged all Christians to love the Rosary and say it fervently."—*The Rosary, My Treasure,* Benedictine Convent, Clyde, Mo.

The Novena consists of five decades of the Rosary each day for twenty-seven days *in petition;* then immediately five decades each day for twenty-seven days *in thanksgiving, whether or not the request has been granted.*

The meditations vary from day to day. On the first day meditate on the Joyful Mysteries; on the second day the Sorrowful Mysteries; on the third day the Glorious Mysteries; on the fourth day meditate again on the Joyful Mysteries; and so on throughout the fifty-four days.

A laborious Novena, but a *Novena of Love.* You who are sincere will not find it too difficult, if you *really wish* to obtain your request.

Should you not obtain the favor you seek, be assured that the Rosary Queen, who knows what each one stands most in need of, has heard your prayer. You will not have prayed in vain. No prayer ever went unheard. And Our Blessed Lady has *never been known to fail.*

Look upon each Hail Mary as a rare and beautiful rose which you lay at Mary's feet.

These spiritual roses, bound in a wreath with Spiritual Communions, will be a most pleasing and acceptable gift to her, and will bring down upon you special graces.

If you would reach the innermost recesses of her heart, lavishly bedeck your wreath with spiritual diamonds—*holy communions.* Then her joy will be unbounded, and she will open wide the channel of her choicest graces to you.

NOTE

In obedience to the decree of Pope Urban VIII and of other Supreme Pontiffs, the author begs to state that, in regard to what is herein narrated, no higher authority is claimed than that which is due to all authentic human testimony.

PROMISES

Made by the Blessed Virgin to St. Dominic and Blessed Alanus.

1. To all those who will recite my Rosary devoutly, I promise my special protection and very great graces.

2. Those who will persevere in the recitation of my Rosary shall receive some signal grace.

3. The Rosary shall be a very powerful armor against hell; it shall destroy vice, deliver from sin, and shall dispel heresy.

4. The Rosary shall make virtue and good works flourish, and shall obtain for souls the•

most abundant divine mercies; it shall substitute in hearts love of God for love of the world, elevate them to desire heavenly and eternal goods. Oh, that souls would sanctify themselves by this means!

5. Those who trust themselves to me through the Rosary, shall not perish.

6. Those who will recite my Rosary piously, considering its Mysteries, shall not be overwhelmed by misfortune nor die a bad death. The sinner shall be converted; the just shall grow in grace and become worthy of eternal life.

7. Those truly devoted to my Rosary shall not die without the consolations of the Church, or without grace.

8. Those who will recite my Rosary shall find during their life and at their death the light of God, the fulness of His grace, and shall share in the merits of the blessed.

9. I will deliver very promptly from purgatory the souls devoted to my Rosary.

10. The true children of my Rosary shall enjoy great glory in heaven.

11. *What you ask through my Rosary, you shall obtain.*

12. Those who propagate my Rosary shall obtain through me aid in all their necessities.

13. I have obtained from my Son that all the confrères of the Rosary shall have for their brethren in life and death the saints of heaven.

14. Those who recite my Rosary faithfully are all my beloved children, the brothers and sisters of Jesus Christ.

15. Devotion to my Rosary is a special sign of predestination.

THE JOYFUL MYSTERIES

Prayer before the recitation:

In the name of the Father,
and of the Son, and of the
Holy Ghost.
Amen.
Then say:
Hail Mary.

In petition

Hail, Queen of the Most Holy Rosary, my Mother Mary, hail! At thy feet I humbly kneel to offer thee a Crown of Roses—snow-white buds to remind thee of thy joys—each bud recalling to thee a holy mystery; each ten bound together with my petition for a particular grace.

O Holy Queen, dispenser of God's graces, and Mother of all who invoke thee! thou canst not look upon my gift and fail to see its binding. As thou receivest my gift, so wilt thou receive my petition; from thy bounty thou wilt give me the favor I so earnestly and trustingly seek.

I despair of nothing that I ask of thee. Show thyself my Mother!

In thanksgiving

Hail, Queen of the Most Holy Rosary, my Mother Mary, hail! At thy feet I gratefully kneel to offer thee a Crown of Roses—snow-white buds to remind thee of thy joys—each bud recalling to thee a holy mystery; each ten bound together with my petition for a particular grace.

O Holy Queen, dispenser of God's graces, and Mother of all who invoke thee! thou canst not look upon my gift and fail to see its binding. As thou receivest my gift, so wilt thou receive my thanksgiving; from thy bounty thou hast given me the favor I so earnestly and trustingly sought.

I despaired not of what I asked of thee, and thou hast truly shown thyself my Mother.

Creed, Our Father, 3 Hail Marys, Glory be to the Father.

I
THE ANNUNCIATION

Sweet Mother Mary, meditating on the Mystery of the Annunciation, when the angel Gabriel appeared to thee with the tidings that thou wert to become the Mother of God; greeting thee with that sublime salutation, "Hail, full of grace! the Lord is with thee!" and thou didst humbly submit thyself to the will of the Father, responding: "Behold the handmaid of the Lord. Be it done unto me according to thy word,"

I humbly pray:

> *Our Father*, *10 Hail Marys*,
> *Glory be to the Father*.

I bind these snow-white buds with a petition for the virtue of

HUMILITY

and humbly lay this bouquet at thy feet.

©

II
THE VISITATION

Sweet Mother Mary, meditating on the Mystery of the Visitation, when, upon thy visit to thy holy cousin, Elizabeth, she greeted thee with the prophetic utterance, "Blessed art thou among women, and blessed is the fruit of thy womb!" and thou didst answer with that canticle of canticles, the Magnificat,

I humbly pray:

> *Our Father, 10 Hail Marys,*
> *Glory be to the Father.*

I bind these snow-white buds with a petition for the virtue of

CHARITY

and humbly lay this bouquet at thy feet.

©

III
THE NATIVITY

Sweet Mother Mary, meditating on the Mystery of the Nativity of Our Lord, when, thy time being completed, thou didst bring forth, O holy Virgin, the Redeemer of the world in a stable at Bethlehem; whereupon choirs of angels filled the heavens with their exultant song of praise—"Glory to God in the highest, and on earth peace to men of good will,"

I humbly pray:

> *Our Father, 10 Hail Marys,*
> *Glory be to the Father.*

I bind these snow-white buds with a petition for the virtue of

DETACHMENT FROM THE WORLD

and humbly lay this bouquet at thy feet.

©

IV

THE PRESENTATION
(*Sometimes called the Purification*)

Sweet Mother Mary, meditating on the Mystery of the Presentation, when, in obedience to the Law of Moses, thou didst present thy Child in the Temple, where the holy prophet Simeon, taking the Child in his arms, offered thanks to God for sparing him to look upon his Saviour and foretold thy sufferings by the words: "Thy soul also a sword shall pierce . . ."

I humbly pray:

> *Our Father, 10 Hail Marys,*
> *Glory be to the Father.*

I bind these snow-white buds with a petition for the virtue of

PURITY

and humbly lay this bouquet at thy feet.

©

V

THE FINDING OF THE CHILD JESUS IN THE TEMPLE

Sweet Mother Mary, meditating on the Mystery of the Finding of the Child Jesus in the Temple, when, having sought Him for three days, sorrowing, thy heart was gladdened upon finding him in the Temple speaking to the doctors; and when, upon thy request, He obediently returned home with thee,

I humbly pray:

> *Our Father, 10 Hail Marys, Glory be to the Father.*

I bind these snow-white buds with a petition for the virtue of

OBEDIENCE TO THE WILL OF GOD

and humbly lay this bouquet at thy feet.

Spiritual Communion, page 43

THE SORROWFUL MYSTERIES

Prayer before the recitation:

In the name of the Father, and
of the Son, and of the Holy
Ghost. Amen. Hail Mary.

In petition

Hail, Queen of the Most Holy Rosary, my
Mother Mary, hail! At thy feet I humbly
kneel to offer thee a Crown of Roses — blood-
red roses to remind thee of the passion of
thy divine Son, with Whom thou didst so
fully partake of its bitterness — each rose recalling to thee a holy mystery; each ten
bound together with my petition for a particular grace.

O Holy Queen, dispenser of God's graces,
and Mother of all who invoke thee! Thou

canst not look upon my gift and fail to see its binding. As thou receivest my gift, so wilt thou receive my petition; from thy bounty thou wilt give me the favor I so earnestly and trustingly seek.

I despair of nothing that I ask of thee. Show thyself my Mother!

In thanksgiving

Hail, Queen of the Most Holy Rosary, my Mother Mary, hail! At thy feet I gratefully kneel to offer thee a Crown of Roses—blood-red roses to remind thee of the passion of thy divine Son, with Whom thou didst so fully partake of its bitterness—each rose recalling to thee a holy mystery; each ten bound together with my petition for a particular grace.

O Holy Queen, dispenser of God's graces, and Mother of all who invoke thee! thou canst not look upon my gift and fail to see its binding. As thou receivest my gift, so wilt thou receive my thanksgiving; from thy bounty thou hast given me the favor I so earnestly and trustingly sought.

I despaired not of what I asked of thee, and thou hast truly shown thyself my Mother.

Creed, Our Father, 3 Hail Marys, Glory be to the Father.

©

I

THE AGONY

O most sorrowful Mother Mary, meditating on the Mystery of the Agony of Our Lord in the Garden, when, in the grotto of the Garden of Olives, Jesus saw the sins of the world unfolded before Him by Satan, who sought to dissuade Him from the sacrifice He was about to make; when, His soul shrinking from the sight, and His precious blood flowing from every pore at the vision of the torture and death He was to undergo, thy own sufferings, dear Mother, the future sufferings of His Church, and His own sufferings in the Blessed Sacrament, He cried in anguish, "Abba! Father! if it be possible, let this chalice pass from Me!"; but, immediately resigning Himself to His Father's will, He prayed, "Not as I will, but as Thou wilt!"

I humbly pray:

*Our Father, 10 Hail Marys,
Glory be to the Father.*

I bind these blood-red roses with a petition for the virtue of

RESIGNATION TO THE WILL OF GOD

and humbly lay this bouquet at thy feet.

©

II
THE SCOURGING

O most sorrowful Mother Mary, meditating on the Mystery of the Scourging of Our Lord, when, at Pilate's command, thy divine Son, stripped of His garments and bound to a pillar, was lacerated from head to foot with cruel scourges and His flesh torn away until His mortified body could bear no more,

I humbly pray:

> *Our Father, 10 Hail Marys,*
> *Glory be to the Father.*

I bind these blood-red roses with a petition for the virtue of

MORTIFICATION

and humbly lay this bouquet at thy feet.

©

III

THE CROWNING WITH THORNS

O most sorrowful Mother Mary, meditating on the Mystery of the Crowning of Our Lord with thorns, when, the soldiers, binding about His head a crown of sharp thorns, showered blows upon it, driving the thorns deeply into His head; then, in mock adoration, knelt before Him, crying, "Hail, King of the Jews!"

I humbly pray:

> *Our Father, 10 Hail Marys,*
> *Glory be to the Father.*

I bind these blood-red roses with a petition for the virtue of

HUMILITY

and humbly lay this bouquet at thy feet.

©

IV

THE CARRYING OF THE CROSS

O most sorrowful Mother Mary, meditating on the Mystery of the Carrying of the Cross, when, with the heavy wood of the cross upon His shoulders, thy divine Son was dragged, weak and suffering, yet patient, through the streets, amidst the revilements of the people, to Calvary; falling often, but urged along by the cruel blows of His executioners,

I humbly pray:

> *Our Father, 10 Hail Marys,*
> *Glory be to the Father.*

I bind these blood-red roses with a petition for the virtue of

PATIENCE IN ADVERSITY

and humbly lay this bouquet at thy feet.

©

V

THE CRUCIFIXION

O most sorrowful Mother Mary, meditating on the Mystery of the Crucifixion, when, having been stripped of His garments, thy divine Son was nailed to the cross, upon which He died after three hours of indescribable agony, during which time He begged from His Father forgiveness for His enemies,

I humbly pray:

Our Father, 10 Hail Marys,
Glory be to the Father.

I bind these blood-red roses with a petition for the virtue of

LOVE OF OUR ENEMIES

and humbly lay this bouquet at thy feet.

Spiritual communion, page 43

THE GLORIOUS MYSTERIES

Prayer before the recitation:

Sign of the cross.

Hail Mary.

In petition

Hail, Queen of the Most Holy Rosary, my Mother Mary, hail! At thy feet I humbly kneel to offer thee a Crown of Roses—full-blown white roses, tinged with the red of the passion, to remind thee of thy glories, fruits of the sufferings of thy Son and thee—each rose recalling to thee a holy mystery; each ten bound together with my petition for a particular grace.

O Holy Queen, dispenser of God's graces, and Mother of all who invoke thee! Thou canst not look upon my gift and fail to see its binding. As thou receivest my gift, so wilt thou receive my petition; from thy bounty thou wilt give me the favor I so earnestly and trustingly seek.

I despair of nothing that I ask of thee. Show thyself my Mother!

In thanksgiving

Hail! Queen of the Most Holy Rosary, my Mother Mary, hail! At thy feet I gratefully kneel to offer thee a Crown of Roses—full-blown white roses, tinged with the red of the passion, to remind thee of thy glories, fruits of the sufferings of thy Son and thee—each rose recalling to thee a holy mystery; each ten bound together with my petition for a particular grace.

O Holy Queen, dispenser of God's graces, and Mother of all who invoke thee! thou canst not look upon my gift and fail to see its binding. As thou receivest my gift, so wilt thou receive my thanksgiving; from thy bounty thou hast given me the favor I so earnestly and trustingly sought.

I despaired not of what I asked of thee, and thou hast truly shown thyself my Mother.

Creed, Our Father, 3 Hail Marys, Glory be to the Father.

I

THE RESURRECTION

O glorious Mother Mary, meditating on the Mystery of the Resurrection of Our Lord from the Dead, when, on the morning of the third day after His death and burial, He arose from the dead and appeared to thee, dear Mother, and filled thy heart with unspeakable joy; then appeared to the holy women, and to His disciples, who adored Him as their risen God,

I humbly pray:

> *Our Father, 10 Hail Marys,*
> *Glory be to the Father.*

I bind these full-blown roses with a petition for the virtue of

FAITH

and humbly lay this bouquet at thy feet.

©

II
THE ASCENSION

O glorious Mother Mary, meditating on the Mystery of the Ascension, when thy divine Son, after forty days on earth, went to Mount Olivet accompanied by His disciples and thee, where all adored Him for the last time, after which He promised to remain with them until the end of the world; then, extending His pierced hands over all in a last blessing, he ascended before their eyes into heaven,

I humbly pray;

> *Our Father, 10 Hail Marys,*
> *Glory be to the Father.*

I bind these full-blown roses with a petition for the virtue of

HOPE

and humbly lay this bouquet at thy feet.

(c)

III

THE DESCENT OF THE HOLY GHOST

O glorious Mother Mary, meditating on the Mystery of the Descent of the Holy Ghost, when, the apostles being assembled with thee in a house in Jerusalem, the Holy Spirit descended upon them in the form of fiery tongues, inflaming the hearts of the apostles with the fire of divine love, teaching them all truths, giving to them the gift of tongues, and, filling thee with the plenitude of His grace, inspired thee to pray for the apostles and the first Christians,

I humbly pray:

> *Our Father, 10 Hail Marys,*
> *Glory be to the Father.*

I bind these full-blown roses with a petition for the virtue of

CHARITY

and humbly lay this bouquet at thy feet.

©

Page Forty

IV

THE ASSUMPTION OF OUR BLESSED MOTHER INTO HEAVEN

O glorious Mother Mary, meditating on the Mystery of Thy Assumption into Heaven, when, consumed with the desire to be united with thy divine Son in heaven, thy soul departed from thy body and united itself to Him, Who, out of the excessive love He bore for thee, His Mother, whose virginal body was His first tabernacle, took that body into heaven and there, amidst the acclaims of the angels and saints, reinfused into it thy soul.

I humbly pray:

> *Our Father, 10 Hail Marys,*
> *Glory be to the Father.*

I bind these full-blown roses with a petition for the virtue of

UNION WITH CHRIST

and humbly lay this bouquet at thy feet.

©

V

THE CORONATION OF OUR BLESSED MOTHER IN HEAVEN AS ITS QUEEN

O glorious Mother Mary, meditating on the Mystery of Thy Coronation in Heaven, when, upon being taken up to heaven after thy death, thou wert triply crowned as the august Queen of Heaven by God the Father as His beloved Daughter, by God the Son as His dearest Mother, and by God the Holy Ghost as His chosen Spouse; the most perfect adorer of the Blessed Trinity, pleading our cause as our most powerful and merciful Mother, through thee,

I humbly pray:

> *Our Father, 10 Hail Marys,*
> *Glory be to the Father.*

I bind these full-blown roses with a petition for the virtue of

UNION WITH THEE

and humbly lay this bouquet at thy feet.

SPIRITUAL COMMUNION

MY JESUS, really present in the most holy Sacrament of the Altar, since I cannot now receive Thee under the sacramental veil, I beseech Thee, with a heart full of love and longing, to come spiritually into my soul through the immaculate heart of Thy most holy Mother, and abide with me forever; Thou in me, and I in Thee, in time and in eternity, in Mary.

In petition

Sweet Mother Mary, I offer thee this Spiritual Communion to bind my bouquets in a wreath to place upon thy brow.

O my Mother! look with favor upon my gift, and in thy love obtain for me (*specify request*) Hail, Mary, etc.

In thanksgiving

Sweet Mother Mary, I offer thee this Spiritual Communion to bind my bouquets in a wreath to place upon thy brow in thanksgiving for (*specify request*) which thou in thy love hast obtained for me. Hail, Mary, etc.

PRAYER

O God! Whose only-begotten Son, by His life, death, and resurrection, has purchased for us the reward of eternal life; grant, we beseech Thee, that, meditating upon these mysteries of the Most Holy Rosary of the Blessed Virgin Mary, we may imitate what they contain and obtain what they promise. Through the same Christ our Lord. Amen.

May the divine assistance remain always with us. Amen. And may the souls of the faithful departed, through the mercy of God, rest in peace. Amen.

Holy Virgin, with thy loving Child, thy blessing give to us this day (*night*).

In the name of the Father, and of the Son, and of the Holy Ghost. Amen.

NOVENA RECORD

In Petition

1 J	2 S	3 G	4 J	5 S	6 G	7 J	8 S	9 G
10 J	11 S	12 G	13 J	14 S	15 G	16 J	17 S	18 G
19 J	20 S	21 G	22 J	23 S	24 G	25 J	26 S	27 G

In Thanksgiving

1 J	2 S	3 G	4 J	5 S	6 G	7 J	8 S	9 G
10 J	11 S	12 G	13 J	14 S	15 G	16 J	17 S	18 G
19 J	20 S	21 G	22 J	23 S	24 G	25 J	26 S	27 G

My Rosary Prayers

THE SIGN OF THE CROSS

In the name of the Father, and of the Son, and of the Holy Ghost. Amen.

THE APOSTLES' CREED

I believe in God, the Father Almighty, Creator of heaven and earth; and in Jesus Christ, His only Son, our Lord: Who was conceived by the Holy Ghost, born of the Virgin Mary, suffered under Pontius Pilate, was crucified, died, and was buried. He descended into hell: the third day He arose again from the dead; He ascended into heaven, sitteth at the right hand of God, the Father Almighty; from thence He shall come to judge the living and the dead. I believe in the Holy Ghost, the holy Catholic Church, the communion of saints, the forgiveness of sins, the resurrection of the body, and life everlasting. Amen.

OUR FATHER

Our Father, Who art in heaven, hallowed be Thy name. Thy kingdom come; Thy will be done on earth, as it is in heaven. Give us this day our daily bread; and forgive us our trespasses, as we forgive those who trespass against us. And lead us not into temptation; but deliver us from evil. Amen.

THE HAIL MARY

Hail, Mary, full of grace; the Lord is with thee; blessed art thou among women, and blessed is the fruit of thy womb, Jesus. Holy Mary, Mother of God, pray for us sinners, now and at the hour of our death. Amen.

GLORY BE TO THE FATHER

Glory be to the Father, and to the Son, and to the Holy Ghost. As it was in the beginning is now, and ever shall be, world without end. Amen.

HAIL, HOLY QUEEN

Hail, holy queen, mother of mercy, our life, our sweetness, and our hope! To thee do we cry, poor banished children of Eve, to thee do we send up our sighs, mourning and weeping in this valley of tears. Turn then, most gracious advocate, thine eyes of mercy toward us; and after this our exile show unto us the blessed fruit of thy womb, Jesus. O clement, O loving, O sweet Virgin Mary!

P. Pray for us, O holy mother of God.

R. That we may be made worthy of the promises of Christ.

The Family Rosary

THE daily practice of this devotion in the family group, father, mother, and children, will serve to create more harmony in the family and will result in greater peace and contentment. It will further increase piety and a greater spiritual development as well as bring down the blessing of God and the watchful care of Our Blessed Lady on all who participate in its daily recitation.

It is also simple to say, and the most convenient time so that all the family might be present is in the evening, probably right after supper. Each member could alternate in leading the prayers.

1. First the Apostles Creed is said while holding the crucifix. The leader would say: "I believe in God," then all would join in the Creed.

2. The leader would then say the first half of the Our Father on the large bead and the first part of the Hail Mary on the three small beads, followed by the Glory be to the Father, while the others recite the second parts of these prayers.

3. The leader then announces: The Five Joyful (or Sorrowful, or Glorious) Mysteries and the name of the First Mystery.

4. Then in order, the Our Father is said on each large bead and the Hail Mary on the small beads as above, with the Glory be at the end of each ten Hail Mary's.

5. Concluding the last decade with the Hail Holy Queen.